The Good Song

An English-French Edition

With an extant excerpt, in appendix, of
"Chapter VII: Marriage – *The Good Song* (1869-1871)" from
Edmond Lepelletier's biography *Paul Verlaine: His Life, His Work*.

Paul Verlaine
"The Prince of Poets"

Translated by Richard Robinson

Sunny Lou Publishing Company
Portland, Oregon, USA
http://www.sunnyloupublishing.com

1st Edition, Revised and Corrected: January 31, 2024
Original Publication Date: May 30, 2022

ISBN: 978-1-955392-28-0

# # #

This translation of *The Good Song* from French is based on the Léon Vanier, Libraire-Éditeur edition of *La Bonne Chanson,* Paris, 1892.

In appendix, the translation of "Chapter VII: Marriage – *The Good Song* (1869-1871)," pp. 208-246, from French is based on the Société du Mercure de France's third edition of *Paul Verlaine: Sa Vie, Son Œuvre* by Edmond Lepelletier, Paris, 1908.

Contents

Foreword

Sed ut perspiciatis, unde omnis iste natus error sit voluptatem accusantium doloremque laudantium, totam rem aperiam eaque ipsa, quae ab illo inventore veritatis et quasi architecto beatae vitae dicta sunt, explicabo. Nemo enim ipsam voluptatem, quia voluptas sit, aspernatur aut odit aut fugit, sed quia consequuntur magni dolores eos, qui ratione voluptatem sequi nesciunt, neque porro quisquam est, qui dolorem ipsum, quia dolor sit, amet, consectetur, adipisci velit, sed quia non numquam eius modi tempora incidunt, ut labore et dolore magnam aliquam quaerat voluptatem. Ut enim ad minima veniam, quis nostrum exercitationemullam corporis suscipit laboriosam, nisi ut aliquid ex ea commodi consequatur? Quis autem vel eum iure reprehenderit, qui in ea voluptate velit esse, quam nihil molestiae consequatur, vel illum, qui dolorem eum fugiat, quo voluptas nulla pariatur? [33] At vero eos et accusamus et iusto odio dignissimos ducimus, qui blanditiis praesentium voluptatum deleniti atque corrupti, quos dolores et quas molestias excepturi sint, obcaecati cupiditate non provident, similique sunt in culpa, qui officia deserunt mollitia animi, id est laborum et dolorum fuga. Et harum quidem rerum facilis est et expedita distinctio. Nam libero tempore, cum soluta nobis est eligendi optio, cumque nihil impedit, quo minus id, quod maxime placeat, facere possimus, omnis voluptas assumenda est, omnis dolor repellendus. Temporibus autem quibusdam et aut officiis debitis aut rerum necessitatibus saepe eveniet, ut et voluptates repudiandae sint et molestiae non recusandae. Itaque earum rerum hic tenetur a sapiente delectus, ut aut reiciendis voluptatibus maiores alias consequatur aut perferendis doloribus asperiores repellat.

– Cicero, 45 BC (*de Finibus Bonorum et Malorum*)

The Good Song

I. The morning sun

The morning sun gently warms and gilds
The still humid ears of rye and wheat,
And the air has kept its coolness overnight.
One exits with no purpose but to exit; one passes
Along the river with its waves of golden grasses,
Down a stretch of lawn that borders ancient alders.
The atmosphere is brisk. At moments, a bird flies
With some hedge fruit or straw in its beak.
And its reflection in the water its passage survives.
That's it.
       But the dreamer loves this landscape
Whose gentle light has suddenly caressed
His dream of adorable happiness and cradled
His delightful memory of that young lady,
Pale apparition who sings and who scintillates,
Whom the poet dreams of and the man cherishes,
Evoking in his wishes, which some might smile at,
The Companion that he finally found, and the soul
That his soul forever yearns for and craves.

II. With every grace and nuance

With every grace and nuance
In the sweet splendor of her sixteen years,
She has the candor of children
And their innocent carousels.

Her eyes are the eyes of an angel
But know, unconsciously,
How to awaken the strange desire
Of an immaterial kiss.

And her hand, in that small place
Where a humming bird would not keep,
Captive, without hope of escape,
Is a heart taken by her in secret.

With her, intelligence comes
In aid of a noble soul; she is
As pure as she is spiritual:
Whatever she says, it was needed!

And if inanity amuses her
And makes her laugh heartlessly,
She would be, being the muse,
Clémente unto friendship,

Unto love – who knows? maybe,
As far as the poet, taken with her,
Who might even beg under her window, –
How audacious! – a worthwhile price

For his song, good or bad!
But testifying, sincerely,
Without *fadaise* and without false note,
To the sweet malaise suffered in love.

III. In a gray and green dress

In a gray and green dress with ruches,
One day in June when I was anxious,
She appeared smiling to my eyes
Which admired her without fear of ambushes;

She came, went, came back again, sat, spoke,
Light and serious, ironical, touched:
And I felt in my darkened soul
As if a joyous reflection of all that;

Her voice, being finely musical,
Deliciously accompanied
The sweet spirit of her charming prattle
Wherein a good heart's gaiety was divined.

So suddenly was I, after the semblance
Of an immediately repressed mutiny,
In full possession of that little Faery
Whom since then I supplicate trembling.

IV. As the dawn grows brighter

As the dawn grows brighter, as behold the aurora!
As hope, after having fled me for a long time, really wants
To come back to me, who call it and who implore it,
As all this happiness really wants to be mine,

My mournful thoughts, they are behind me now,
They are behind me my bad dreams, ah! they are behind me
Above all the irony and pursed lips
And the words wherein my soulless mind triumphed.

Behind me also are my clenched fists and anger
With respect to the jerks and rascals I've encountered;
Behind me abominable rancor! behind me
The oblivion one seeks in execrable drinks!

For I want, — now that a Being of light
Has emitted that clarity, in my deep night,
Of a love both immortal and primary,
Through grace, smiles, and loyalty, —

I want, guided by you, bright eyes with sweet flames,
Led by you, o hand that my hand trembles in,
To walk straight, be that over moss-covered paths
Or rocks and pebbles that encumber the way;

Yes, I want to walk straight and calm in Life,
To the place where fate will lead my steps,
Without violence, without remorse, without envy.
It will be the happy duty in gay combats.

And as, to offset the slownesses of the journey,
I will sing some ingenuous tunes, I tell myself
She will hear me without displeasure doubtless;
And, really, I desire no other Paradise.

V. Before you go, pale star

Before you go,
Pale star of morning,
          – A thousand quail
Are singing, singing in the thyme. –

Turn towards the poet,
Whose eyes are filled with love,
          – The lark
Is climbing to heaven with the dawn. –

Turn your gaze which drowns
The aurora in its azure;
          – What a joy
To be among fields of ripe wheat! –

Then make my thought shine
Over there, – quite far, oh, quite far away!
          – As the dew
Is gaily gleaming on the hay. –

In the gentle dream where
My sweetheart stirs, still asleep...
          – Quick, quick,
For here comes the golden sun. –

VI. The pale moon shines

The pale moon
Shines in the woods;
From each bough
Emerges a voice
Beneath the branches...

O beloved...

The pond reflects,
Profound mirror,
The silhouette
Of a dark willow
Where the wind weeps...

Let's dream, it is the hour,

A vast and tender
Appeasement
Seems to descend
From the firmament
That the star iridesces...

It is the exquisite hour.

VII. The scene framed by the curtains

The scene framed by the curtains
Runs furiously by, and entire plains
With water, wheat, trees, and sky
Hurtle towards the cruel tourbillon
Wherein thin telegraph poles fall
Whose wires look like paraphs, strangely.

An odor of coal burning and water boiling,
All the noise that a thousand chains make, at the end
Of which a thousand giants hurl, when whipped;
And all of a sudden, an owl's prolonged cries. –

– What is all that to me, when I have before my eyes
The pale vision that makes my heart joyous,
For her sweet voice still rings in my ears,
For the Name, so beautiful, noble, and sonorous,
Pure pivot to all that swirling, mixes in
With the rhythm of the brutal wagon, smoothly.

VIII. A Saint in her aureole

A Saint in her aureole
A Chatelaine in her tower,
All that the human word
Contains of grace and love;

The golden note that a horn
Makes in the distant wood,
Married to the tender pride
Of noble Ladies of yesteryear;

With that, the distinguished charm
Of a fresh, triumphant smile
Wrapped in cygnet candors
And a child-wife's blushes;

A gentle patrician accord
Of nacreous aspects, pink and white.
I see, I hear, all these notes
In her Carolingian name.

IX. Her right arm

Her right arm, in an adorably sweet gesture,
Rests around her little sister's neck,
While her left arm follows the rhythm of her skirt.
Doubtless, an agreeable idea entertains her,
For her frank eyes, her smiling mouth,
Testify to an intimate and spirited joy.
Oh! her exquisite and fine thought, what is it?
So very cute, so very lovable and beautiful, –
For this portrait, her infallible taste has chosen
Also the best and simplest of poses:
Standing, eyes forward, no hat; and her dress
Just long enough for her to hide, halfway,
Under its jealous folds, the charming toes
Of an imperceptibly mischievous foot.

X. Fifteen long days still

Fifteen long days still, and more than six weeks,
Already! Without a doubt, among human anguishes,
The most painful anguish is that of being separated.

One writes, one speaks one's love; one makes an effort
Each day to evoke the voice, the eyes, the gestures
Of the person in whom one puts one's joy, and one stays
For hours talking to the absent one, all alone.
But everything one thinks, and everything one feels,
And everything one says to the absent one, continues
To remain pale and faithfully sad.

Oh! The absence! the least clement of all evils!
To console oneself with phrases and words,
To dip into the bottomless morosity of thoughts
To refresh oneself, finding nothing more than tired hopes,
Nothing more than what is wan and bitter!
And then look, – penetrating and cold like steel,
Rapider than birds and bullets and than the gusts
Of wind blown southerly from across the sea
And bearing on its sharp tip a fine poison;
See how it comes, like an arrow, the suspicion
Shot by impure and lamentable Doubt.

Is it really true? With elbows on the table,
I read your letter, tears in my eyes,
Your letter, wherein is expressed a delicious avowal, –
Is she not, then, distracted by other things?
Who knows? While here, for me, the days move slow
And morose like a river past a withered shore,
Perhaps her innocent lips have parted and smile?
Perhaps she is very joyous and forgets me?

I reread her letter with melancholy.

XI. The difficult trial will end soon

The difficult trial will end soon:
My heart, smile at the future.

The days of alarm have passed
When I was sad to tears.

No more counting the instants,
My soul, the time is near.

I have silenced bitter expressions
And banished somber chimeras.

My eyes, exiled from seeing her,
On account of grievous duty,

My ears, avid to hear
The golden notes of her sweet voice, –

All my being and all my love
Acclaim the happy day

When, my only dream and thought, –
The fiancée will return to me!

XII. Go, song, at the speed of flight

Go, song, at the speed of flight,
Go before her and tell her that,
Though in my faithful heart
There is a joyous ray

Dissipating, with a sacred light,
These tenebrae of love:
Fear, doubt, mistrust,
And behold the day has come!

Fearful and silent for a long time, –
Do you hear it? Gaiety
Like a lively lark
In the clear sky has sung.

Go then, ingenuous song,
And, without vain regret,
Let her be the welcome one,
The one who returns finally.

XIII. Yesterday, we spoke of many things

Yesterday, we spoke of many things,
And my eyes went searching yours;

And your eyes went searching mine
While our conversation proceeded

Under the banality of weighty expressions
My love followed after your thoughts;

And when you spoke distractedly
I lent an ear to your secret:

For the voice, as well as the eyes, of Her
Who makes you joyous, discovers you sad

Despite every morose and laughable effort,
And shines a light on your inner being.

Now, yesterday I departed intoxicated:
Is it an empty hope that my heart caresses,

A vain hope, false and sweet companion?
Oh! no! right? that is not right, no?

XIV. The hearth, the narrow light of the lamp

The hearth, the narrow light of the lamp;
The revery with a finger against the temple
And the eyes losing themselves in the beloved's;
The hour of piping hot tea and closed books;
The sweetness of sensing the end of the evening;
The charming fatigue and the adored expectation
Of nuptial shade and sweet night,
Oh! all that, my softened dream pursues it
Relentlessly, through every vain postponement,
Impatient for the months, furious for the weeks!

XV. I am almost afraid, to be honest

I am almost afraid, to be honest,
So much do I feel my life intertwined
With the radious thought
That possessed my soul last summer,

So much does your image, forever cherished,
Reside in this heart that is entirely yours,
My heart uniquely anxious
To love you and please you;

And I tremble, pardon me
For saying so, for speaking so frankly,
To think that a word, a smile
From you is always my law now,

And that all it would take from you is
A gesture, a word, or a blink of the eye,
To throw all my person into mourning
For that celestial illusion.

But I don't want to see you, in any other way, –
The future would need be too dark for me
And fecund in innumerable sorrows, –
Than through an immense hope,

Immersed in that supreme happiness
Of your telling me forever and again,
In spite of my dismal returns,
That "I *love* you," that "I love *you*"![1]

---

[1]That I love you (twice): the French accusative case of "vous" (formal "you") and "te" (informal "you") is almost untranslatable in modern English. "Thee" for the formal "you," would work, but also sounds odd to the modern ear. So we have resorted for repetition and emphasis instead.

XVI. The noisy cabarets

The noisy cabarets, the dirty sidewalks,
The plane trees stripped of leaves in a dark atmosphere,
The omnibus, a hurricane of old iron and muck,
Which squeals, poorly resting on its four wheels,
And rolls its eyes, green and red, slowly,
With laborers going to the club, all smoking
Their tobacco pipe under the nose of police agents,
Cascading roofs, sweating walls, slippery pavements,
Torn-up asphalt, streams overflowing the sewer,
And there you have my route, – with paradise in view.

XVII. Isn't that right? In spite of the sots

Isn't that right? In spite of the sots and wicked people
Who will not fail to envy our joy,
We will be proud sometimes and always indulgent.

Isn't that right? We will go, gaily and slowly,
In the modest way that smiling Hope points out to us,
Little concerned that one sees us or does not see us.

Isolated in our love as in a dark wood,
Our two hearts, exhaling their peaceable tenderness,
Will be two nightingales singing in the evening.

As for the World, whether it be irascible towards us
Or sweet, what do its actions matter? It can,
If it likes, caress us or use us for target practice.

United by the strongest and the dearest tie,
And, moreover, possessing adamantine armor,
We will smile at everyone and have nothing to fear.

Without concerning ourselves with what our Fate
Has in store for us, we will walk at the same pace
And hand in hand, with the childish spirit

Of those who love innocently, isn't that right?

XVIII. We are in infamous times

We are in infamous times
Wherein the marriage of souls
Must seal the union of hearts;
At this hour of frightful storms
Twice the courage is not too much
To live under such vanquishers.

In the face of what one dares,
It would be proper for us, in all things,
To stand up, an couple ravished
In the austere ecstasy of the just,
And proclaiming, with an august gesture,
Our proud love, like a defiance!

But what need is there to say it to you?
You the goodness, you the smile,
Are you not also the counsel,
The good advice, loyal and brave,
A child smiling at the thought that is grave,
To which all my heart says: thank you!

XIX. So, that will be on a bright summer day

So, that will be on a bright summer day:
The great sun, an accomplice to my joy,
Will make, among the silk and satin cloth,
Your dear beauty more beautiful still;

The all-blue sky, like a tall tent,
Will shiver sumptuously along its folds
Over our two happy faces that the emotion
Of joy and expectation makes pallid.

And when evening comes, the air will be soft
Which will play, caressingly, in the canvas,
And the peaceful appearance of stars
Will smile benevolently on the two spouses.

XX. I was going along perfidious paths

I was going along perfidious paths
Dolorously uncertain.
Your dear hands were my guides.

So pale on the distant horizon,
A feeble hope of dawn shined;
Your look was the morning.

No sound, unless his sonorous pace,
Encouraged the traveller.
Your voice said to me: "Keep walking!"

But my fearful heart, my dark heart,
Wept alone along that sad path;
Love, the delicious victor,

Reunited us in joy.

XXI. The winter has ceased; the light is warm

The winter has ceased; the light is warm
And it dances from the ground to the bright firmament.
The saddest heart must cede
To the immense joy dispersed through the air.

Even this sullen and ill Paris
Seems to welcome young suns
And as if for an immense accolade
Extends a thousand arms from its vermillion roofs.

I have, for a year now, springtime in my soul,
And the green return of a sweet floreal,
Just like a flame surrounding a flame,
Stacks the ideal upon my ideal.

The blue sky prolongs, raises, and crowns
The unmovable azure where my love smiles.
The season is gorgeous, and my role is good,
And all my hopes have their turn finally.

Let summer come! Let autumn and winter
Come too! And each season will be
Charming to me, o You whom
This fantasy and this reason adorn!

La Bonne Chanson
(French)

I. Le soleil du matin

Le soleil du matin doucement chauffe et dore.
Les seigles et les blés tout humides encore,
Et l'azur a gardé sa fraîcheur de la nuit.
L'on sort sans autre but que de sortir; on suit,
Le long de la rivière aux vagues herbes jaunes,
Un chemin de gazon que bordent de vieux aunes.
L'air est vif. Par moments un oiseau vole avec
Quelque fruit de la haie ou quelque paille au bec,
Et son reflet dans l'eau survit à son passage.
C'est tout.
       Mais le songeur aime ce paysage
Dont la claire douceur a soudain caressé
Son rêve de bonheur adorable, et bercé
Le souvenir charmant de cette jeune fille,
Blanche apparition qui chante et qui scintille,
Dont rêve le poète et que l'homme chérit,
Évoquant en ses voeux dont peut-être on sourit
La Compagne qu'enfin il a trouvée, et l'âme
Que son âme depuis toujours pleure et réclame.

II. Toute grâce et toutes nuances

Toute grâce et toutes nuances
Dans l'éclat doux de ses seize ans,
Elle a la candeur des enfances
Et les manèges innocents.

Ses yeux qui sont les yeux d'un ange,
Savent pourtant, sans y penser,
Éveiller le désir étrange
D'un immatériel baiser.

Et sa main, à ce point petite
Qu'un oiseau-mouche n'y tiendrait,
Captive, sans espoir de fuite,
Le coeur pris par elle en secret.

L'intelligence vient chez elle
En aide à l'âme noble; elle est
Pure autant que spirituelle:
Ce qu'elle a dit, il le fallait!

Et si la sottise l'amuse
Et la fait rire sans pitié,
Elle serait, étant la muse,
Clémente jusqu'à l'amitié.

Jusqu'à l'amour – qui sait? peut-être,
A l'égard d'un poète épris
Qui mendierait sous sa fenêtre,
L'audacieux! un digne prix

De sa chanson bonne ou mauvaise!
Mais témoignant sincèrement,
Sans fausse note, et sans fadaise,
Du doux mal qu'on souffre en aimant.

III. En robe grise

En robe grise et verte avec des ruches,
Un jour de juin que j'étais soucieux,
Elle apparut souriante à mes yeux
Qui l'admiraient sans redouter d'embûches;

Elle alla, vint, revint, s'assit, parla,
Légère et grave, ironique, attendrie:
Et je sentais en mon âme assombrie
Comme un joyeux reflet de tout cela;

Sa voix, étant de la musique fine,
Accompagnait délicieusement
L'esprit sans fiel de son babil charmant
Où la gaîté d'un coeur bon se devine.

Aussi soudain fus-je, après le semblant
D'une révolte aussitôt étouffée,
Au plein pouvoir de la petite Fée
Que depuis lors je supplie en tremblant.

IV. Puisque l'autre grandit

Puisque l'aube grandit, puisque voici l'aurore,
Puisque, après m'avoir fui longtemps, l'espoir veut bien
Revoler devers moi qui l'appelle et l'implore,
Puisque tout ce bonheur veut bien être le mien,

C'en est fait à présent des funestes pensées,
C'en est fait des mauvais rêves, ah! c'en est fait
Surtout de l'ironie et des lèvres pincées
Et des mots où l'esprit sans l'âme triomphait.

Arrière aussi les poings crispés et la colère
A propos des méchants et des sots rencontrés;
Arrière la rancune abominable! arrière
L'oubli qu'on cherche en des breuvages exécrés!

Car je veux, maintenant qu'un Être de lumière
A dans ma nuit profonde émis cette clarté
D'une amour à la fois immortelle et première,
De par la grâce, le sourire et la bonté,

Je veux, guidé par vous, beaux yeux aux flammes douces,
Par toi conduit, ô main où tremblera ma main,
Marcher droit, que ce soit par des sentiers de mousses
Ou que rocs et cailloux encombrent le chemin;

Oui, je veux marcher droit et calme dans la Vie,
Vers le but où le sort dirigera mes pas,
Sans violence, sans remords et sans envie.
Ce sera le devoir heureux aux gais combats.

Et comme, pour bercer les lenteurs de la route,
Je chanterai des airs ingénus, je me dis
Qu'elle m'écoutera sans déplaisir sans doute;
Et vraiment je ne veux pas d'autre Paradis.

V. Avant que tu ne t'en ailles

Avant que tu ne t'en ailles,
Pâle étoile du matin,
        – Mille cailles
Chantent, chantent dans le thym. –

Tourne devers le poète,
Dont les yeux sont pleins d'amour,
        – L'alouette
Monte au ciel avec le jour. –

Tourne ton regard que noie
L'aurore dans son azur;
        – Quelle joie
Parmi les champs de blé mûr! –

Puis fais luire ma pensée
Là-bas, – bien loin, oh! bien loin!
        – La rosée
Gaîment brille sur le foin. –

Dans le doux rêve où s'agite
Ma vie endormie encor...
        – Vite, vite,
Car voici le soleil d'or. –

VI. La lune blanche

La lune blanche
Luit dans les bois;
De chaque branche
Part une voix
Sous la ramée...

O bien-aimée.

L'étang reflète,
Profond miroir,
La silhouette
Du saule noir
Où le vent pleure...

Rêvons, c'est l'heure.

Un vaste et tendre
Apaisement
Semble descendre
Du firmament
Que l'astre irise...

C'est l'heure exquise.

VII. Le paysage dans le cadre des portières

Le paysage dans le cadre des portières
Court furieusement, et des plaines entières
Avec de l'eau, des blés, des arbres et du ciel
Vont s'engouffrant parmi le tourbillon cruel
Où tombent les poteaux minces du télégraphe
Dont les fils ont l'allure étrange d'un paraphe.

Une odeur de charbon qui brûle et d'eau qui bout,
Tout le bruit que feraient mille chaînes au bout
Desquelles hurleraient mille géants qu'on fouette;
Et tout à coup des cris prolongés de chouette. –

– Que me fait tout cela, puisque j'ai dans les yeux
La blanche vision qui fait mon coeur joyeux,
Puisque la douce voix pour moi murmure encore,
Puisque le Nom si beau, si noble et si sonore
Se mêle, pur pivot de tout ce tournoiement,
Au rythme du wagon brutal, suavement.

VIII. Une Sainte en son auréole

Une Sainte en son auréole,
Une Châtelaine en sa tour.
Tout ce que contient la parole
Humaine de grâce et d'amour;

La note d'or que fait entendre
Un cor dans le lointain des bois,
Mariée à la fierté tendre
Des nobles Dames d'autrefois!

Avec cela le charme insigne
D'un frais sourire triomphant
Éclos dans des candeurs de cygne
Et des rougeurs de femme-enfant;

Des aspects nacrés, blancs et roses,
Un doux accord patricien.
Je vois, j'entends toutes ces choses
Dans son nom Carlovingien.

IX. Son bras droi

Son bras droit, dans un geste aimable de douceur,
Repose autour du cou de la petite soeur,
Et son bras gauche suit le rythme de la jupe.
A cour sûr une idée agréable l'occupe,
Car ses yeux si francs, car sa bouche qui sourit,
Témoignent d'une joie intime avec esprit.
Oh! sa pensée exquise et fine, quelle est-elle?
Toute mignonne, tout aimable, et toute belle,
Pour ce portrait, son goût infaillible a choisi
La pose la plus simple et la meilleure aussi:
Debout, le regard droit, en cheveux; et sa robe
Est longue juste assez pour qu'elle ne dérobe
Qu'à moitié sous ses plis jaloux le bout charmant
D'un pied malicieux imperceptiblement.

X. Quinze longs jours encore

Quinze longs jours encore et plus de six semaines
Déjà! Certes, parmi les angoisses humaines
La plus dolente angoisse est celle d'être loin.

On s'écrit, on se dit comme on s'aime; on a soin
D'évoquer chaque jour la voix, les yeux, le geste
De l'être en qui l'on mit son bonheur, et l'on reste
Des heures à causer tout seul avec l'absent.
Mais tout ce que l'on pense et tout ce que l'on sent,
Et tout ce dont on parle avec l'absent, persiste
A demeurer blafard et fidèlement triste.

Oh! l'absence! le moins clément de tous les maux!
Se consoler avec des phrases et des mots,
Puiser dans l'infini morose des pensées
De quoi vous rafraîchir, espérances lassées,
Et n'en rien remonter que de fade et d'amer!
Puis voici, pénétrant et froid comme le fer,
Plus rapide que les oiseaux et que les balles
Et que le vent du sud en mer et ses rafales
Et portant sur sa pointe aiguë un fin poison,
Voici venir, pareil aux flèches, le soupçon
Décoché par le Doute impur et lamentable.

Est-ce bien vrai? tandis qu'accoudé sur ma table
Je lis sa lettre avec des larmes dans les yeux,
Sa lettre, où s'étale un aveu délicieux,
N'est-elle pas alors distraite en d'autres choses?
Qui sait? Pendant qu'ici, pour moi, lents et moroses
Coulent les jours, ainsi qu'un fleuve au bord flétri,
Peut-être que sa lèvre innocente a souri?
Peut-être qu'elle est très joyeuse et qu'elle oublie?

Et je relis sa lettre avec mélancolie.

XI. La dure épreuve va finir

La dure épreuve va finir:
Mon coeur, souris à l'avenir.

Ils sont passés les jours d'alarmes
Où j'étais triste jusqu'aux larmes.

Ne suppute plus les instants,
Mon âme, encore un peu de temps.

J'ai lu les paroles amères
Et banni les sombres chimères.

Mes yeux exilés de la voir
De par un douloureux devoir,

Mon oreille avide d'entendre
Les notes d'or de sa voix tendre,

Tout mon être et tout mon amour
Acclament le bienheureux jour

Où, seul rêve et seule pensée,
Me reviendra la fiancée!

XII. Va, chanson, à tire-d'aile

Va, chanson, à tire-d'aile
Au-devant d'elle, et dis-lui
Bien que dans mon coeur fidèle
Un rayon joyeux a lui,

Dissipant, lumière sainte,
Ces ténèbres de l'amour:
Méfiance, doute, crainte,
Et que voici le grand jour!

Longtemps craintive et muette,
Entendez-vous? la gaîté
Comme une vive alouette
Dans le ciel clair a chanté.

Va donc, chanson ingénue,
Et que, sans nul regret vain,
Elle soit la bienvenue
Celle qui revient enfin.

XIII. Hier, on parlait de choses

Hier, on parlait de choses et d'autres,
Et mes yeux allaient recherchant les vôtres,

Et votre regard recherchait le mien
Tandis que courait toujours l'entretien.

Sous le sens banal des phrases pesées
Mon amour errait après vos pensées;

Et quand vous parliez, à dessein distrait
Je prêtais l'oreille à votre secret:

Car la voix, ainsi que les yeux de Celle
Qui vous fait joyeux et triste décèle,

Malgré tout effort morose et rieur,
Et met en plein jour l'être intérieur.

Or, hier, je suis parti plein d'ivresse:
Est-ce un espoir vain que mon coeur carresse,

Un vain espoir, faux et doux compagnon?
Oh! non! n'est-ce pas? n'est-ce pas que non?

XIV. Le foyer, la lueur étroite de la lampe

Le foyer, la lueur étroite de la lampe;
La rêverie avec le doigt contre la tempe
Et les yeux se perdant parmi les yeux aimés;
L'heure du thé fumant et des livres fermés;
La douceur de sentir la fin de la soirée;
La fatigue charmante et l'attente adorée
De l'ombre nuptiale et de la douce nuit,
Oh! tout cela, mon rêve attendri le poursuit
Sans relâche, à travers toutes remises vaines,
Impatient des mois, furieux des semaines!

XV. J'ai presque peur, en vérité

J'ai presque peur, en vérité,
Tant je sens ma vie enlacée
A la radieuse pensée
Qui m'a pris l'âme l'autre été,

Tant votre image, à jamais chère,
Habite en coeur tout à vous,
Mon coeur uniquement jaloux
De vous aimer et de vous plaire;

Et je tremble, pardonnez-moi
D'aussi franchement vous le dire,
A penser qu'un mot, un sourire
De vous est désormais ma loi,

Et qu'il vous suffirait d'un geste,
D'une parole ou d'un clin d'oeil,
Pour mettre tout mon être en deuil
De son illusion céleste.

Mais plutôt je ne veux vous voir,
L'avenir dût-il m'être sombre
Et fécond en peines sans nombre,
Qu'à travers un immense espoir,

Plongé dans ce bonheur suprême
De me dire encore et toujours,
En dépit des mornes retours,
Que je vous aime, que je t'aime!

XVI. Le bruit des cabarets

Le bruit des cabarets, la fange des trottoirs,
Les platanes déchus s'effeuillant dans l'air noir,
L'omnibus, ouragan de ferraille et de boues,
Qui grince, mal assis entre ses quatres roues.
Et roule ses yeux verts et rouges lentement,
Les ouvriers allant au club, tout en fumant
Leur brûle-gueule au nez des agents de police,
Toits qui dégouttent, murs suintants, pavé qui glisse,
Bitume défoncé, ruisseaux comblant l'égout,
Voilà ma route – avec le paradis au bout.

XVII. N'est-ce pas? en dépit des sots

N'est-ce pas? en dépit des sots et des méchants
Qui ne manqueront pas d'envier notre joie,
Nous serons fiers parfois et toujours indulgents

N'est-ce pas? nous irons, gais et lents, dans la voie
Modeste que nous montre en souriant l'Espoir,
Peu soucieux qu'on nous ignore ou qu'on nous voie.

Isolés dans l'amour ainsi qu'en un bois noir,
Nos deux coeurs, exhalant leur tendresse paisible,
Seront deux rossignols qui chantent dans le soir.

Quant au Monde, qu'il soit envers nous irascible
Ou doux, que nous feront ses gestes? Il peut bien
S'il veut, nous caresser ou nous prendre pour cible.

Unis par le plus fort et le plus cher lien,
Et d'ailleurs, possédant l'armure adamantine,
Nous sourirons à tous et n'aurons peur de rien.

Sans nous préoccuper de ce que nous destine
Le Sort, nous marcherons pourtant du même pas,
Et la main dans la main, avec l'âme enfantine

De ceux qui s'aiment sans mélange, n'est-ce pas?

XVIII. Nous sommes en des temps infâmes

Nous sommes en des temps infâmes
Où le mariage des âmes
Doit sceller l'union des coeurs;
A cette heure d'affreux orages,
Ce n'est pas trop de deux courages
Pour vivre sous de tels vainqueurs.

En face de ce que l'on ose
Il nous siérait, sur toute chose,
De nous dresser, couple ravi
Dans l'extase austère du juste
Et proclamant, d'un geste auguste
Notre amour fier, comme un défi!

Mais quel besoin de te le dire?
Toi la bonté, toi le sourire,
N'es-tu pas le conseil aussi,
Le bon conseil loyal et brave,
Enfant rieuse au penser grave,
A qui tout mon coeur dit: merci!

XIX. Donc, ce sera par un clair jour d'été

Donc, ce sera par un clair jour d'été:
Le grand soleil, complice de ma joie,
Fera, parmi le satin et la soie,
Plus belle encore votre chère beauté;

Le ciel tout bleu, comme une haute lente,
Frissonnera somptueux à longs plis
Sur nos deux fronts heureux qu'auront pâlis
L'émotion du bonheur et l'attente;

Et quand le soir viendra, l'air sera doux
Qui se jouera, caressant, dans vos voiles,
Et les regards paisibles des étoiles
Bienveillamment souriront aux époux.

XX. J'allais par des chemins perfides

J'allais par des chemins perfides,
Douloureusement incertain.
Vos chères mains furent mes guides.

Si pâle à l'horizon lointain
Luisait un faible espoir d'aurore;
Votre regard fut le matin.

Nul bruit, sinon son pas sonore,
N'encourageait le voyageur.
Votre voix me dit: «Marche encore!»

Mon coeur craintif, mon sombre coeur
Pleurait, seul, sur la triste voie;
L'amour, délicieux vainqueur,

Nous a réunis dans la joie.

XXI. L'hiver a cessé: la lumière est tiède

L'hiver a cessé: la lumière est tiède
Et danse, du sol au firmament clair.
Il faut que le coeur le plus triste cède
A l'immense joie éparse dans l'air.

Même ce Paris maussade et malade
Semble faire accueil aux jeunes soleils
Et, comme pour une immense accolade,
Tend les mille bras de ses toits vermeils.

J'ai depuis un an le printemps dans l'âme
Et le vert retour du doux floréal,
Ainsi qu'une flamme entoure une flamme,
Met de l'idéal sur mon idéal.

Le ciel bleu prolonge, exhausse et couronne
L'immuable azur où rit mon amour.
La saison est belle et ma part est bonne,
Et tous mes espoirs ont enfin leur tour.

Que vienne l'été! que viennent encore
L'automne et l'hiver! Et chaque saison
Me sera charmante, ô Toi que décore
Cette fantaisie et cette raison!

Appendix

The following text is taken extant from "Chapter VII: Marriage – *The Good Song* (1869-1871)," pp. 208-246, of *Paul Verlaine: His Life, His Work*, by Edmond Lepelletier. Third Edition, Société du Mercure de France, Paris, 1908.

Chapter VII: Marriage – *The Good Song* (1869-1871)

Verlaine hadn't had a single veritable event in his life. He passed his existence in the margins of the great things, and even the small things, of his time. Republican, he did not get mixed up in any of the conspiring projects [to overthrow the imperialistic government], none of the agitations, none of the student moments that were so frequent during the last years of the Empire. He did not participate in the so-called "Cafe of the Renaissance" affair. He, who did not hold cafes in horror, never frequented the Brasserie Serpente, nor the Brasserie Glaser, nor even the Cafe de Madrid, places where youth hostile to the imperial regime congregated, and where one was exposed to violent altercations, trials like that of the *Treize* (Thirteen), to arbitrary arrests, perquisitions, charges by police agents, and even preventative imprisonment in Mazas, followed by a trial for plotting [against the government] and high treason before the High Court, presiding at Blois. He frequented, without mixing in, in the milieu of all those political hotbeds. Although a patriot, he did not make war except from afar, almost like a spectator, and he mounted guard so to speak from an armchair. Although living in Paris, during the terrible siege, he did not take any part in the actions in the public square. Under the Commune, he was a silent and inactive figure in the formidable drama, and his pencil-pushing at Hôtel de Ville, where he remained peaceably camped, could not be compared to a barricade. He never mixed in, at least until *Invectives*, in the pointed literary polemics of his times; he never took part in a duel. As with everyone else, he experienced cruel losses in his family, his father to begin with, his cousin Elisa; then his excellent mother set his heart in mourning, but those are regular catastrophes, which one anticipates, and which are part and parcel of the baggage of miseries of human life.

If he succumbed at the denouement, it was not at all because of a sudden, unexpected debacle, but after a series of monetary outlays that succeeded, one after the other, in addition to the quotidian expenses of existence and maintenance, costs of trips and repeated payments for his pleasures and the satisfaction of his pleasures. Without a renewal of capital, without an intake of fixed receipts and serious resources proceeding from regular work, in the end he had zero. He ate, like another La Fontaine, his foundation and its revenue. He descended instead, and each day a little bit more, all the steps of the ladder of distress. He had, moreover, losses of money to submit to as a result of engagements, contracts, failed enterprises, like his agricultural adventures in Juniville and in Coulommes. A swindle on the part of an abbot deprived him of his last cash. But his progressive ruin was not due to those great and terrible commotions that shocked an entire existence; they were calculated so to speak, and while acknowledging that he could have prevented his last ecus from being taken by the abbot Salard, he could have, all the same, declared bankruptcy within a month's time after that.

A single event dominated his entire destiny, filled it, perturbed it, poisoned it: that was his marriage.

It is impossible to reconstruct the life of a man after the fact. It would be ridiculous to want to draw a horoscope after a person is dead; and it would be folly, reconstructing, piece by piece, a destiny, to try to imagine a Verlaine who remained a bachelor and stayed employed at an office job, regularly receiving a wage, living bourgeoisement with his good mother, leading, until the last days of that excellent woman's life, a relatively regular existence, with visits to the banal Venus mixed in, sittings in cafes, then, serenely, satisfied, sober, appeased, writing at his leisure, in the quietude of his home office, in the isolation of his bedroom, or under the refreshment of green fronds, poems more or less researched and chiseled, grouped together in some reviews that have artistic pretensions. A wisened Verlaine, level-headed, correct, wearing clothes purchased at la Belle Jardinière,[2] a regular contributor to journals, a laureate in the Académie Française, after having led a sinecurist and monotonous life finally, but happy and soft, together with some of his childhood comrades, terminating their careers in a good administrative arm-

[2]La Belle Jardinière: a kind of department store of fashion, rather like the Galeries Lafayettes today.

chair, like Albert Mérat, or better still in a chair at the Institute, like José-Maria de Heredia, librarian to boot.

Perhaps, if his destiny had been thus channeled, if the torrent of his life had flowed regularly and peaceably, within the smooth walls of an administrative career, if he had never lost his familial habits, Verlaine would have continued to write good poems, in the objective and descriptive manner of Leconte de Lisle. He would not have been the strange, sensational, so personally vibrant poet with the shudderings of a man skinned alive, who made a shiver run up and down our spine by his unpublished art, and who created something of a new poetic, a poetry unknown until him.

Perhaps, if all his misfortunes originate in his marriage, everything that made his personality, his originality, everything that assures him a place apart in the egalitarian assembly of poets, perhaps the glory that illumines his tomb, – it would all have no other source than that same marriage. Verlaine, if he had remained a bachelor, would have been an esteemed, as well as respectable poet, but that is all.

No matter who his wife was, marriage for him would not have been happy, not even possible, in spite of his having said, notably in the famous poem of *Songs Without Words*, "You did not have enough patience..."

The poet's bad destiny is not then imputable to the choice even of her whom he took for a companion, but a conjugal union which he was not at all cut out for, with his excitable temperament, his passionate exuberance, the deplorable facility by which he let himself be led, turned around, embroiled in bad ways.

Lots of young people marry for love, to possess the desired person who rejects their solicitations without legal consecration, or because of family suitability, interest, calculation, or to maintain a situation where the quality of being a married man is useful, requisite even, in order to possess an establishment where the man must be accompanied, seconded, or also because one is tired of the bachelor's life, furnished hotels, bachelor pads with domestic tyrants, greasy spoons, chance mistresses, and finally, in order to settle down, to have a home, children, a family, to base one's life on solid foundations and fix one's existence forever. But those motives, which are more or less exclusively the same for all men, young or old, who seek marriage, were probably very far from the brusque decision that Verlaine made.

He doubtless loved the young girl whose appearance made so vivid an impression on him, and he himself recounted how he felt the traditional lightning strike, but what made him decide to marry was above all a feeling, in the terrain of love, of personal humility and inferiority, which he felt was his lot by nature.

His marriage, or rather his somewhat sudden, extravagant, decision, which resembled a temerarious and sometimes preposterous determination, made while intoxicated, decided on at the drop of a hat, to request the hand in marriage (and it was to her half-brother, a young man without familial authority, that he made his request) of a girl, whom he had only spoken to for several minutes, was like a protestation by the poet against the random injustice of physiognomy, like a defiance to the fatality of a physical constitution.

Verlaine, it must be repeated, was afflicted by an intense ugliness. When he got older, his unsightly and bizarre physiognomy, asymmetric with his lumpy head and his pug nose, appeared supportable enough. One saw it burning with the brightness of intelligence, and aureoled by a beaming of talent. One got used to his faun-like mask, when he laughed, and his sinister aspect, when he remained serious. His jerky features, his jutting jaws, with the salient zygomas, his features recalling that classic death head, presented a special hideousness, which, in certain respects, could attract interest and even please. But, in his youth, he was of a grotesque ugliness; he resembled, not a mongoloid, as has been said, but an ape, and his baboon-like originality could not inspire in a woman he met anything but a feeling of repulsion, repugnance, maybe even fright and disgust. If I insist on those physical particularities it is because criticism, but also philosophy and history, attach too little importance to the sexual life. Historians, psychologists, moralists annoyingly look down on the formidable role of the genetic element in the human drama.

The poor fellow knew quite well the repugnant effect he produced; he freely joked about his "rascal-like physique," and he cast off, at random moments, on the covers of notebooks, in the margin of volumes, silhouettes, drawings, and designs, which affirmed the notion he had of his lack of corporeal advantages. He proved to be a pitiless caricaturist of himself.

He also felt timid and awkward with respect to women. He had none of those ingenuous flirts, none of those charming intrigues at twenty years old, which are often, for those who do not write verse, all the poetry they experience in life. One saw, in the letter dated September 1862 from Lécluse, that he did not fail to attach interest to those first innocent contacts with the pretty sex. He wrote about the contra dance he participated in with the daughter of the instructor, Mlle. Hiolle. But that quadrille had no follow up. He did not come away from the dance with a smile or a promise to see one another again, and he was downcast, gloomy, disappointed, wishing to remove from his thoughts the young person who showed no desire whatsoever in approaching him again. He felt separated from women by an abyss, a recluse who can never have access to love, nor the presumption of encountering it, because of the improbability or at least inadmissibility. One does not fall in love with a queen unless one is part of her entourage or is one of her domestics, like Ruy Blas, and the postillion Bergami.

Coming from someone who did not lose sight of him for a single day in the eight years proceeding his marriage, I do not believe that Paul ever planned any love affair, that he ever even attempted to court a woman whomever she might be, a *grisette* on the street, a sweetheart, or a female artist met in literary milieux; if he had, he would certainly have spoken to me about it, or I would have found out his secret.

The occasions, however, were not lacking of course. To Mme. de Ricard's salon came young women who had had adventures, and half-honest girls; in the more joyous house of Mme. de Callias, amiable and sufficiently easy women were encountered. He could have found himself, like all men, on promenades, at soirees, in the theater, at concerts, on trips, in the chance presence of desirable

creatures, pleasing to him, with whom he could have struck up a re-
lationship which would have had the ordinary denouement. It was
not the case with him.

He never had, in his youth, a mistress, in the sense of an
amorous continuity or in a purely sensual sense, – that is, a real, reg-
ular woman, with or without a husband, lover, protector, adorers –
who passed, if not exclusively, at least by preference, by tenderness,
or, if you like, by interest for his own. He did not even frequent easy
women regularly, as a customer, as a temporary and intermittent
lover, as often happens. His amorous adventures were of the most
ordinary simplicity: he betook himself only to those miserable
wretches who sell love like a commodity item. He went to drink of
caresses, as if of absinthe, at the first counter that he came across on
a street corner. He himself recounted, later, with his ingenuous cyni-
cism, how the first fruits of his youth were sacrificed, in a house of
prostitution, demolished today, on the rue d'Orléans-Saint-Honoré.

He had, therefore, never been in love, and his first poetry
owed doubtless to that lack of passion, desires, combats, and suffer-
ing also, an ideality, an impassiveness that few poets before him had,
and which, with marriage, he was soon bound to lose.

It is very rare, in fact, that a poet should reach twenty-five
years of age and not have been in love, not have sung his hopes, his
dreams, his sensations, his jealousies, his triumphs, his traversed be-
trayals, and his worst suspicions.

Every man is or has been a poet in that sense, and each of us
keeps, in a perfumed corner of his memory, the confused and always
secretly admired image of some vanished, effaced, almost unreal
Beatrice, who had existed for several instants only, who very often
never suspected the tenacious and artificial passion that she had in-
spired in him in passing. We all have, more or less, lived through the
sonnet d'Arvers.[3]

Verlaine did not know those ecstasies, those desires, those
joys and those sorrows of first loves, so often vivid and unfortunate.
He had no idea, in the hour of springtime, of the revenges and the

---

[3]Sonnet d'Arvers: *Un secret*, a sonnet written by Félix Arvers (AD 1806-1850).

reprisals of the heart that succeed discouragement, at that moment of terrible annihilation when the loved woman escapes, and when one believes that the entire world is going to crumble on its foundations, because a corsage is tightened or a skirt is lowered. He did not experience those alternations of felicity and sadness that are all part of the realities of love, the sensual spasm being quite frankly an illusion, given, without the smitten cerebrality of identity, it would be the same everywhere, the same satisfaction everywhere.

I never saw Verlaine, in his youth, give his arm to a woman. He never spoke to me about engaging in one of those charming parties of two, sometimes four, six or eight even, which leave such gay memories! I often went boating, Sundays, on Joinville-le-Point; he never wanted to accompany me. It wasn't however the canoe, nor the countryside, nor the bottles of wine under the arbors that displeased him. He felt alone, without a companion, and hardly ever counted on a chance meeting during one of those parties. He had no knowledge of those crazy groups that dispersed while singing refrains, alternately foolish, obscene, or sentimental, alongside hedges, accompanied by the culling of violets or blackberries, depending on the season. He took no part in gay repasts in the dancehalls of Montmartre, on the Butte, or in Montrouge or Châtillon. However, I introduced him once into a society of young men who held their sessions at the dancehalls in Montmartre, at the Elysée, at the Château-Rouge. That group, which went by the name of *The Collective*, a cooperative society of drinking and pleasure, hardly pleased him; he contented himself with looking at us amuse ourselves, laughing, dancing, pinching waists and rubbing bosoms. He emptied, conscientiously and alone, the cups, while we diverted ourselves with the crazy regulars of the joint, who came and sat down beside us, out of breath and red in the face, after a jolting quadrille or a breathless waltz. He appeared to my friends, journalists and employees at the bourse or in commerce, a rather lugubrious convive, and one of those among us, the future explorer Louis Advenant, said to him, on leaving: "You don't have a crazy bone in your body! When I have a hiccough, I'll come and find you!"

He kept to himself for the most part, under the excitation of repeated aperitifs, either in special establishments, which he has shamelessly called his fields of passionate exploits, establishments of love of the third order, moreover, with reduced tariffs, or among the poor girls, spiders of pleasure, watching from their windows, behind a lamp, the passerby disposed to getting himself caught in their curtains. Verlaine wanted nobody for a companion on those adventures. He told me, but only rarely and by exception, about his peripeteia, always the same, and in which he took no pride rightly. Love did not exist for him then, in his twentieth year, but under the form of a physical need, a sensual satisfaction of the coarsest kind, and that great idealist was nothing but the most materialist of lovers.

But one day, chance placed him in the presence of a young girl, a real young girl, almost a child, Mlle. Mathilde Mauté de Fleurville.

It was in that house on rue Nicolet, in Montmartre, which was going to become for him the theater of so many intimate dramas, where he found himself face to face with the heroine, with his Destiny made woman.

He had gone to see the composer Charles de Sivry, who lived there, at the house of his step-father, M. Mauté de Fleurville, with his mother, married for a second time to the said M. Mauté, an old notary from the countryside, the perfect type of a bourgeois, with short sideburns and gold-rimmed eyeglasses.

Someone knocked at the door of the room where Sivry and his visitor were chatting. Oh! that joyous and profound knock knock! It must have echoed in the poet's soul forever after that!

A young girl appeared, dressed in gray and green, with ruches, a attractive brunette...

Verlaine has deliciously painted that charming apparition in these lines:

> *In a gray and green dress with ruches,*
> *One day in June when I was anxious,*
> *She appeared smiling to my eyes*
> *Which admired her without fear of ambushes;*

She came, went, came back again, sat, spoke,
Light and serious, ironical, touched:
And I felt in my darkened soul
As if a joyous reflection of all that;

Her voice, being finely musical,
Deliciously accompanied
The sweet spirit of her charming prattle
Wherein a good heart's gaiety was divined.

So suddenly was I, after the semblance
Of an immediately repressed mutiny,
In full possession of that little Faery
Whom since then I supplicate trembling.

His first conversation with her was simple and decisive. Curiosity must have doubtless compelled the young girl towards her brother's room. She passed her little eavesdropping head through the half-opened door, and pretended to retire with light and confused protestations and amiable grimaces.

"Stay then!" said Charles... "Monsieur is a poet... it's Verlaine... you know Verlaine?"

One had, in fact, often spoke about him in the Mauté household. I have mentioned, earlier, what plans for operettas were preoccupying Verlaine at that time. Charles de Sivry, future head of the orchestra at the Chat Noir, was on the lookout for a funambulesque poem [to put] to music. He was envisioning *Petit Faust* and *Belle Hélène*. Moreover, Sivry was a regular at Nina's soirées,[4] and of course, on multiple occasions, Charles had spoken, with his mother, about the people he met at that talked-about house, frequented by interesting personalities, on their way to becoming famous. He had even brought home the poet's works, the *Poems Saturnian* and *The Fêtes Galantes*. The young girl must have cast an indiscreet eye over those verses, in a permitted reading, without much interest to her otherwise.

---

[4]Nina: for more on Nina and her soirées, see *Ten Years a Bohemian* by Émile Goudeau.

At her brother's invitation, Mlle. Mauté stayed then, and the conversation interested her. She said to Verlaine that she loved his poetry, even though they appeared a bit hard to her, and the poet, touched in his self-esteem as an author, was also touched by another feeling.

It seemed to him, – was it an illusion? it is very possible that it was not one, – that this young girl was looking at him differently than the majority of women he'd met before, that she did not fix on him two ironic, disdainful, cruel, insolent or frightened eyes, with those disparaging looks that he saw in all the pupils that his desire had searched. The young girl did not seem to have any fear of him. Hadn't she noticed his hideousness? After all, perhaps he did not appear as ugly to her as he seemed to himself? Was that compassionate child considering him with more indulgent eyes than other persons of the same sex, than his friends, than himself? Was it by chance?....

He dared not go to the extreme of the too flattering supposition, but a sufficiently favorable prejudice seized his mind, and he considered that young girl strangely, who several instants earlier only was unknown to him, ignored, unsuspected, greeted with indifference. He examined her with profound attention, while she, from his point of view, seemed to observe him on the sly, not without some interest. He was not just anyone, and he merited that some attention should be paid to him, he thought, vainly. That advantageous hypothesis would accelerate the working of his brain, where a new love, impulsive, penetrating, without warning! shook everything.

What chemist, in a subtle crucible, has ever analyzed human feelings so completely as to be able to give us the composition of the distillation of the sensual, intellectual, volitional, or purely instinctive parts that one calls love? Materialistic philosophers have claimed that the instinct of a living being, that the desire to perpetuate the race, and the obligation for a woman and a man to come together, with a view to accomplishing the ends of nature, which are the continuation of the species, have the decisive part in what is called sympathy, attraction, desire, choice, an irresistible penchant. Man and woman, put into each other's presence, would be attracted uniquely by the imperious feeling, most often unconscious, of the being they carry the germ of inside themselves, and which they must produce by their union.

The special selection that they would make of such encountered subject would explain that phenomenon of amorous identity, that so-violently exclusive preference that would result in the negative result, that quite often a lover will abstain from all carnal commerce, will become unproductive, and will be as if touched by impotence, being unable to accomplish the sexual act with the elect person. Sometimes he will die without wanting to have been satisfied or consoled by any other female, very nearly like magnets however, reciprocally attractive, and physiologically similar to what they want, and what moves away from them. It is that *very nearly like* which is, above and beyond scientific conclusions on the reproduction and perpetuation of the species, what one calls Love.

There was perhaps something like the blooming of a new and unprecedented flower in Verlaine's soul. Until then, his thought had been to distance himself from lively affections. He had grown separate from woman, from the companion with whom he could have, in Schopenhauer's system, entertained the idea of founding a family, and of glimpsing the possibility of engendering a child. He must have known then a confused and new feeling. Whence a sudden enchantment.

From her side, the young girl, subject to the influence of her sex, feeling probably a passing impulse, dominated perhaps by a momentary, but strong excitation, due to the presence of that strange man, felt the secret desire to be his companion, to belong to him. It is certain that at the end of that too brief hour there was, between those two beings, a brief and harmonious, but alas! fleeting, accord.

I can confirm, being a confidant to the intoxication of those initial encounters, those veritable discoveries of the soul, that both were instantly pleased with the other. The classic bolt of lightning never grows old. It continues to stay forever young. The proof of that amorous spontaneity, above all from the young girl's side, is that Mlle. Mathilde Mauté, very young, having consequently the time to find a husband, living as she was in an easy, bourgeois milieu, was in normal conditions and able to take her time to marry, according to familial accords, either an employee, or a functionary, or a business man, or even a man of letters, but without haste. She could wait and choose. She accepted however with a sort of precipitation a marriage which she could have adjourned, dragged out, and refused finally, after reflection and comparison. Nothing seemed to need to draw her to that union, which was ordinary from the point of view of fortune, nothing appeared to compel her to encourage, to provoke, if you will, a cavalier so little seductive as was our friend.

There was, on her part, no calculation of ambition, cupidity, or any desire for independence. She was not pressed to leave the family home, where she was pampered, where she lacked nothing, where she was cherished, adulated, adored. Nor was she a romantic young girl. She already showed a very practical common sense and a very ponderous bourgeois mind, which later she gave strong demonstrations of. There was never any question of her and Verlaine having lost their head. No anticipation had taken place with respect to the permitted treats of nuptials. If however she had been the least prepared in the world for one of those conjugal advances, it is not Verlaine who would have been opposed to it, of course. But she did not allow the lover to grow bold. With precocious sagacity and an ever-present possession of herself, she kept the masculine impatience of her ardent fiancé at bay until the legal hour.

Living in a milieu where one often spoke of literature, where one vaunted artists, hearing her mother, a very good pianist, praise famous men, and her brother, Charles de Sivry, name familiarly the young notorieties which whom he rubbed shoulders, perhaps there was, at the beginning of Verlaine's literary renown which accompanied him, a particular prestige, a favorable attraction to the poet; perhaps also she read in the eyes of that man, whom she saw for the first time, the flames of desire, the attraction of passion, and she was attracted and dominated by the amorous force that he suddenly exuded. Whatever the case, she loved him at first sight, and the union was planned, decided, announced like a veritable marriage of love.

Verlaine has recounted how his encounter with that young girl had turned his life upside down. A moral cyclone. The same day of his first encounter, his habits were so troubled that he forgot, at the cafe du Delta, where Charles de Sivry had rejoined him, to taste his usual green cocktail! Love suppressing the aperitif! That miracle was not bound to be repeated.

Verlaine quit Paris then. He left precipitously, either to give another course to his ideas, or to reason through the nascent love which he felt had invaded him. He left for the North, his refuge, his consolation, and whence he wrote to me this quick note, for he had departed without letting anyone know about it:

> *Fampoux, at M. Julien Déhée's (Pas-de-Calais), near Arras.*
>
> *Great suffering suddenly, departed no less quickly. Letter from my mother to my boss. Details forthcoming, or prompt return, following expected response.*
>
> *Think about the* Forgerons. *Write me. Be well. Your devoted,*
>
> — PAUL VERLAINE
>
> *June 4, 1869.*

In the calm of the countryside, he reasoned with himself, organized his thoughts, took his pulse mentally, found himself very much in love, judged that he had reason to be, and brusquely, perhaps under the influence of some cup which gave him courage, he wrote a long letter to Charles de Sivry. That missive was not abiding by the rules of matrimonial accords. It was found to be little conformant with the usual private rules of protocol that, under similar circumstances, was to be followed in families. Verlaine, of his comrade, bravely asked, a bit brutally also, the hand of his sister. It was not even established whether Charles de Sivry, a young man of great musical talent but without a social situation, nor the authority in the family, moreover only the half-brother of Mlle. Mathilde, was qualified to grant or refuse the little hand asked for.

But Verlaine hardly cared, at that moment of psychic excitation, about questions of familial precedence. He had entirely forgotten about M. Mauté, the father; he had not even thought about the mother, with whom he was not on bad terms. He had written in an excess of fever. He dropped the letter in a box, as if he was getting rid of a compromising piece of paper, and, still under the influence of his febrile passion, returned to his relative Déhée's place, with precipitous step, with a distracted air, with his eyes shining. Without consulting anyone, he threw himself on the bed and slept profoundly, until someone came to wake him to come to the table.

In Déhée's house, they thought that he had emptied a few more cups than usual, and his sleep elicited no commentary from those good folk, being indulgent to the immoderate absorptions of beer or gin.

Soon a letter from Charles de Sivry arrived, the response so impatiently waited for. His future brother-in-law told him that, motivated by the unexpected, and surprised by the unprecedented nature of the request, he had communicated Verlaine's letter to his sister, first! That was a serious inappropriateness as well, but there was nobody to tell them. He had then made the same communication to his mother, who referred it to her husband, M. Mauté. Sivry added this positive word, that there was room "to hope." M. Mauté hardly counted. His wife and daughter approved in principal, that was the important thing. There was then room to believe that all would end for the best. But Paul had to understand that one could not give him an immediate response. It was more than probable that he did not have to fear a refusal.

Sivry encouraged him then to remain several more days in the country. He promised to come and visit him soon, to escort him back to Paris. Then, one would see. Things would probably turn out for the best.

Let's just say, in order to explain, as we did for the young girl, the promptitude with which the family Mauté agreed to the project of marriage, that the Mauté family had two girls, that their fortune was not considerable, and that Verlaine, physical appearances aside, was not a person to disdain. He was not the famished poet of Bohemian legend. Employed at the prefecture of the Seine, he had a serious situation, fixed, solid, very appreciated in the bourgeois world. An employment like that was something to count on. He was a bachelor and, by consequence, he could hope, after taking examinations, to climb the ladder. What's more, an only son, he expected to inherit tens of several thousands of *livres* of rent from his mother, not to mention other relatives, cousins, male and female, whom he was the eventual heir to. Finally, from the first words to Sivry, he had written that he loved Mathilde, and that he would take her as she was. The famous words: *without dowry*! is still the best "Open Sesame" of bourgeois marriages.

Behold Verlaine in seventh heaven. He read and reread the recomforting response. His imagination leaps forward to events: he sees himself already accepted, hopeful, received, loved, a fiancé he is allowed to court. He rejoiced in advance for those approaching acts of marriage. He saw himself finally a spouse, a happy spouse! He learns by heart the happy letter from Sivry, and, in his emotion, he forgets to get drunk. For two days in a row, he was not to be seen at his habitual estaminet. Serious symptom.

Every moment then was an enchantment. A fairytale. Each night, he saw himself in a dream, his foot on that Jacob's ladder of lovers, at the summit of which is the canopy, the canopy assuredly of the bed, because Verlaine's passion, although issuing from an entirely ideal and entirely immaterial sentiment, which I will try to define, ended finally, and he confessed as much himself, in the banal and material conclusion of all unions on this earth: in the bedroom.

In the course of those several weeks of amorous incubation, the poet was subject to passionate hallucination. He wrote as a lover. It is certain that he vehemently desired, loved and adored her who was to become his wife, and whom he has subsequently missed and redesired, but there was in his passion a great deal of the artificial, of the fictive, and one might also say of the artistic. He loved objectively, and Mathilde was merely the representation of a concept of his mind.

We have already said that Verlaine's first relations with women, – and he didn't hide them, – had been vulgar, unworthy, shameful even. Because of that, the end of his amorous career was bound irritatingly to resemble the beginning. He had never experienced an honest love, a pure and real love, in the sense of a feeling that has for its object a person susceptible of inspiring, not only desire, but esteem. He was unfamiliar with passion accompanied by respect. It was like an unknown world opening up before him, that love which was contained by a sort of admiration, as virtue and dignity alone ought to give rise to it. He had never really been loved. He had not experienced the banal vanity that the attention of one of those women procures, in the arms of whom sensuality, and drunkenness sometimes, had thrown him, and which could have borne witness to him, as sometimes happens, of a gross preference: for venal Venus has her caprices and her hours of liberality. He was unable to verify for himself the Latin aphorism, cited by Cicero: *Ab amico amante argentum accipere meretrix non vult.*[5] He knew quite well the practical motives and grateful cupidity of those passive lovers, encountered in random hovels, sought out in red light districts. The feeling that he had of his physical imperfections and the difficulties that he would need to overcome if, feeling passion, he wanted to inspire it, added to that totally new feeling of joy, appreciated, desired even perhaps, by a young girl raised in conditions of candor and complete honorability. What's more, he thought, with vain satisfaction, that he was surely the first man likely to teach that young Mathilde about love. She had not, before him, so much as looked at a man with the thought of becoming his companion. She was so young! as he has said on multiple occasions, – a great quality, and also a grave defect. He would not have to wait long to find out.

As soon as that idea entered into his impressionable brain, that he could be loved by that young girl, that he was susceptible of appearing desirable to a pure, naïve being, with as yet unsuspected feelings, whom he would be the initiator of, the educator of; and like Pygmalion animating his statue, it dominated him. That possibility intoxicated him, stunned him, and suggested to him those hypotheses, those imaginations and those combinations of visions, of situations, as drunkenness likes to construct them. Those suppositions became for him a reality. By dint of envisaging certain phenomena brought together, juxtaposed, constructed in his mind with all the

---

[5] *Ab amico... vult:* Latin for "A prostitute does not wish to accept money from a lover."

rooms, he finished by imagining them to be real. Verlaine, in his countryside solitudes of Pas-de-Calais, while smoking his pipes, while emptying his cups, while wandering amidst the gloomy plains that border the sea of beetroots, and along the melancholic routes bordering the colza, practiced the indisputable theory, established by the scientists of the school of Nancy, of auto-suggestion.

The result was that he became really amorous, and that he found it very simple that he was not repulsed a priori, and that he was loved, desired, as he desired, as he loved.

Then began for him a new series of auto-suggestions. Charles de Sivry came to find him at Fampoux, bringing him the favorable response, already promised, and taken by the lover for granted. He reaffirmed for him his first counsel: that his mother and his sister were disposed to accept the request of M. Paul Verlaine, but a certain amount of time was necessary for reflection, and that it was then necessary to know the opinion of Mme. Verlaine, Paul's mother, for Paul had forgotten to alert his mother to his marital projects. Finally, for two months, the Mauté family was going to sojourn with friends, in Normandy. On return, "one would see." Then one would speak seriously, definitively.

That week, – passed in the company of Charles de Sivry who, in order to distract himself, played the organ on Sundays and practiced his improvisations at the church in Fampoux, as well as ballet tunes and operetta choruses, – only augmented Paul's desire to follow up on the request, given that it was not repulsed and that no serious objection had been brought forward. He came back to Paris with Sivry, and informed his mother. Mme. Verlaine, a little surprised by the unexpected determination of her naughty boy of a son to "put an end to things," to get his ducks in a row, to become a serious man, to establish himself, as one says in Artois, did not show herself to be discontented. The Mauté family, whom she was somewhat familiar with, through my mother, through Mme. Bertaux, appeared suitable to her. She grimaced all the same when Paul told her that there was no dowry to be counted on. But what held the ascendancy in her mind, over every other consideration, was the regular existence that her son was going to lead from then on out. A married man could not continue running off to the estaminets. She had once found Paul one morning lying in his sheets, his top hat completely covered in mud, still on his head. He would certainly assume, thanks to a conjugal life, better habits.

The good mother Verlaine had already observed a notable change in her son. He had disembarked from the wagon without stopping by the cafes near the *gare du Nord*, and embracing her, on his arrival, she had perceived no odor of alcohol. He had remained sober in route, and he was not sick either. Grave subject for surprise.

That happy change continued. During the first period of his return, Verlaine drank less. He had been afraid of being invited to come and pay his respect, without having had the time to dissipate the alcoholic fumes. He had enough consciousness of his weaknesses not to defy circumstances and the natural order of events. He was bound to fear that at a first interview, for the other one had not really counted, he should happen to present himself in a disconcerting state of overexcitement, eyes haggard, jerky movements, coarse voice, after the absorption of multiple aperitifs, which would have been disastrous and would have destroyed forever the scaffolding of happiness that his imagination was building.

He watched his behavior then. He found himself in the situation of the evangelical parable of the Virgins, waiting for the coming of the spouse. He had also become, at work, a more exact employee. His sous-chef paid him some compliments. His absence was noticed at the cafe du Gaz. He returned home at a decent hour on rue Lécluse, and he no longer balked so strongly when his mother proposed to him to accompany her on some visit to a bourgeois family in the Batignolles, where one played bezique, at a sou per two thousands, while drinking tea and eating dry petits-fours.

He was successful however, with the help of Charles de Sivry, in exchanging several letters with the young girl who remained in Normandy. Innocent pages in form and substance, for he watched over his quill as well as his thirst. Mlle. Mauté had announced to him her next return to Paris. She recommended wisdom and patience to him, with an eye to the future. The little person reasoned using a magnificent seriousness. She said that everything was for the best between them: age, taste, education, social class, money even, and she spoke, as if it were a certain thing, very soon, of their common happiness. She made declarations of economy and foresight. She indicated a selection of apartments. A bright lodging, even if located a little higher up off the street, would be better. They were young, they had legs and could walk up stairs. She occupied herself with furnishing the conjugal nest. She thought even about the question of beds. She wanted two, one made of rosewood, stark and simple, for him; the other, for her, with Persian padding, rose or blue.

Verlaine left the decision about the duality of nuptial beds to the side, while remembering "the saintly innocence of his so puerilely good and *zézayante*"[6] fiancée.

Verlaine began then to court her by letters. Acting the gallant in that fashion was most advantageous to him. His epistolary banter was always interesting, humorous, amusing; what's more, rather often than not, he wrote in verse, composing as he went along his sensations, his desires, his impatiences, those delicate and charming stanzas, which he was later bound to collect into a volume of poetry under the title, which became ironic much later, of *The Good Song*.

That poetic labor merely kept alive his mental rutting, fulfilled his cardiac and cerebral inflammation. Composition, the choice of words, the searching for rhymes, all the lyrical effort kept the fire, which he himself had lit, more intense and more devouring; he stoked it febrilely, each day, with the burning poker of his ardent strophes.

Finally, the Mauté family returned from Normandy, and the intensely desired interview took place, rue Nicolet, after dinner. He himself recounted, with good-naturedness, that presentation, where there was always, on both sides, a bit of the conventional and formality. According to tradition, as with every man showing up to a first rendezvous, or to a matrimonial interview, he had paid exceptional attention to his toilette, and his mother had had to make and remake the knot of his Lavallière tie.

---

[6]*zézayante*: refers to a kind of lisping, but particular to the French language wherein a person pronounces "s" instead of "ch" and "z" instead of "j".

Introduced into the salon on rue Nicolet, it was the mother of the young girl who first came forward and encouraged him with a shake of the hand and a smile. She presented him immediately there-after to her husband, M. Mauté. He was an old rural notary, with a red face, with the wily look of a rich person from the country, a good man fundamentally, but very close to his interests, having the interi-or dryness and apparent plumpness of the business man.

Finally, the young Mathilde entered. She was no longer wearing the costume, forever fixed in the poet's verses of *The Good Song*: "the gray and green dress with ruches." Verlaine was so ner-vous that he no longer recalled, afterwards, in what way his fiancée was dressed that day. He was too preoccupied examining her face to notice the fabric of her dress. It was indeed the apparition that had so often haunted his reveries. She was there before him, in the flesh, living and smiling! She appeared to him even more charming, more cute than the first time. The auto-suggestion had worked, but reality surpassed the imaginative vision.

They sat around the table, and they began to chat. They said things of apparent insignificance, but full of promise for both beings, whose destiny was irrevocably weft together. The consent of parents was obtained. The suitor was accepted. From that day forward, every evening, whatever the weather, Verlaine showed up at the house on rue Nicolet.

I have hardly any letters from him during that year. He al-most entirely forgot his companions at the cafe, and his best friends only saw him at brief intervals. He made only rare appearances at Lemerre's; he almost completely stopped his visits to Leconte de Lisle's house, to Banville's house. I frequented him less, going but rarely to visit him at Hôtel de Ville to speak with him, very busy as I was with journalism and political battles, which were very lively at that time. His letters recalled to me only our drama: *The Forgerons*, which had remained on hold, and which marriage and subsequent events were to forever interrupt.

All the while courting, Verlaine continued to rhyme his *Good Song*. That prolonged wait pf nearly one year had overexcited the desires of the young fiancé even more. They were in agreement on matters of mutual interest, on all important points, except on the date of the ceremony. The end of spring or the beginning of summer of 1870 was chosen finally. But again the apologue of the cup and the lips came true: brusquely an illness appeared and, one day as he presented himself on rue Nicolet, smiling as usual, Verlaine found his fiancée in bed: she had the chicken pox. Even though he was of a rather timid and fearful temperament, on this occasion passion took the upper hand and made him bold. He presented himself as temerarious even: despite observations that were made to him, he absolutely had to see the patient. So he entered her room and, after having heard some incoherent words leave the young, feverish mouth which the delirium was agitating, he retired, discouraged, demoralized. The darkest phantoms haunted his path, while he sadly returned to the Batignolles.

The marriage, whose banns had been announced, found itself indefinitely adjourned. He analyzed very closely the feelings of irritation, disappointment, and sorrow that were assailing him at that moment:

In the very real and, like all very real mental or physical sorrow, very chaste sorrow was mixed, I have to admit, a kind of base disappointment, which I blamed myself for and blushed almost, mentally, I dare say, to feel as rather carnal, as it is said. So, there was my marriage pushed out to the indefinite future!... It was a great deal of trouble to abstain for so long, to fast so much!... I was like someone who would be ashamed to find the name to give to abstinence, to fasting, and I was like someone to whom – excuse the vulgar expression used to characterize a vulgar sentiment – one would have promised more butter than bread, and who would have neither bread nor butter.

But finally the malady diminished in intensity, the convalescent reappeared and the marriage was fixed for the first half of July. But then, new setback: the mother was taken ill in turn; the epidemic raged through that house.

Mme. Mauté healed rather rapidly and the marriage was finally settled for the month of August.

Verlaine absented himself for a few days, in order to go to Normandy. He was invited by a very good woman, who wore her heart on her sleeve, not beautiful, but rather of crass manners and appearance, fated later in life for singular adventures which the tribunals made public, for she was despoiled successively by several lovers lacking in scruples, to whom she had imprudently abandoned herself: she was called the marquess de Manoury. Very hospitable, generous, who loved to receive, to host, having a certain fortune; she sought out poets, artists, and above all those who had the Bohemian air: the Normand manor was a veritable annex of Nina's house.

That short absence of one week had been advised to Verlaine, whose impatience redoubled in direct relation to the marriage date's approach, and who became so irritable that some were afraid he might fall ill in turn. Mathilde had asked for a separation of one week, and he docilely obeyed.

During that absence, he wrote numerous letters, wrote a great deal of rhyming verse, the majority of which unfortunately were not included in *The Good Song*, and were lost even. He came back to Paris, to settle the details of his marriage once and for all, which was, in spite of everything, approaching. The legal banns were made, and one had just enough time to deal with the tailor, the seamstress, the jeweler, and also the carpenter and the furnishing of the young couple's household.

But a tragic incident upset the young lover, who had barely returned from the hospitable manor: three days before his marriage, one of our friends, a young writer, one of the hosts of the salon Ricard, Lambert de Roissy, having lost a mistress whom he adored, blew his brains out in Passy. He had informed Verlaine of his fatal decision and made him responsible for diverse arrangements after his death.

As he returned from the burial of that poor comrade, heavy with enervation and depression, Verlaine sat down at a table in the cafe de Madrid, to read the journals and quench his thirst. The city was in a state of febrile and tragic agitation. War had begun seriously, terribly: the first cannons had been fired and already the sinister phantom of the rout raised its head on our invaded frontiers. To make matters worse, a false joy had run through Paris. A fabricated dispatch had announced a great victory: it proclaimed the defeat of the army of the Prince Frédéric-Charles. MacMahon was appointed to command the French army, with cannons and flags taken from the enemy. All the boulevards had been decorated in an instant. Cries of joy mounted in every bosom; along the terraces of the cafes, animated and exalted words spread from table to table. People embraced, they addressed strangers familiarly, and the details of the victory were retold, growing amplified each time they were repeated. "The Prince Frédéric-Charles had been surrounded by the African chasseurs and obliged to surrender." "Not at all!" another narrator said, who appeared to be better informed, "it was the captain So-and-so, of the 4th battalion of the second regiment of such and such infantry!" One gave the number of the victorious regiment, which had surrounded the prince's staff officers. It was to that captain that the prince had had to hand over his sword. Later, the prowess of the Turks was told. In another group, the story of the arrival in Paris of the conquered flags of the enemy... It was counseled to promenade them through the boulevards, before suspending them from the ceiling of the Invalides...

Suddenly, from the Bourse, came the brutal truth: we had been beaten. MacMahon was in full retreat. It was a total disaster, lugubrious presage of future defeats.

Verlaine, who had spent the day before filling out paper work for the commissariat of police and at the city hall in Passy, for the burial of the poor Lambert de Roissy, and a good part of the day at the cemetery, hadn't had time to read the newspapers. He stumbled onto that brouhaha, ignorant of all that was going on around him, not understanding a thing. At the cafe de Madrid, comrades he met had apprised him of the situation, and he was quickly in diapason with the general overexcitement. He may even have surpassed the ambient exaltation, for he had just knocked back, one after the other, two strong aperitifs. A regiment passed on the boulevard: the comrades who had gotten him up to speed, almost all of them journalists of the opposition, began to cry: "Long live the Republic!" We gathered together then at that cafe de Madrid, the meeting presided over by Bouvet, with Delescluze, Charles Quentin, Peyrouton, Jules Ferry, Henry Maret, Lissagaray, and plenty others who have since disappeared or are dead.

Verlaine, standing, cried with the others, sticking out of the crowd with his very tall top hat, the umbrella he was brandishing in one hand, and his mourning attire. A drinker near him apostrophized, saying, "It's 'Long live France!' that one should be crying. We are not a Republic!"

At the same time, that gentleman, who seemed to be a crazed friend of the Empire, pointed the poet out to the agents who made an attempt to seize him.

The regulars of the cafe de Madrid were, fortunately, numerous, and they were prepared to put up a resistance to the sarges, which was at that time almost a daily affair. It was the time of "White Blouses." The police had, one evening, laid siege to the cafe; we were barricaded in with tables and chairs. Resistance was a regular thing. We repulsed, once again, the intervention of police agents, and Verlaine was encouraged, after having been saved from the clutches of the policemen, to slip away as soon as possible, through the passage Jouffroy. He didn't wait to be told a second time, and took off.

He stopped, however, along the way, to down another refreshment, for he was extremely overheated, and then his emotions changed and he bought two evening journals, which had just appeared. His eyes fell on the following news:

The Empress Regent has promulgated, the Counsel of Ministers having been heard, the Legislative Body having voted, and the Senate having been heard, the following law:

All non-married men, of the class 1844-1845, who are not already enlisted, are called to arms.

Verlaine belonged to the class of 1844; he was exempt from service, having furnished a replacement, and being the son of a widow, but the decree was official: he had to enlist! His patriotic sentiments, for the moment, evaporated, and he no longer thought about crying "Long Live the Republic!" nor long live anything whatsoever; and pounding his fist on the table, he cried: "My marriage is f***"d!" And with that, he ordered another absinthe and drank it fiercely.

Now, the marriage was fixed for the following day. He expressed his misgivings to the family of his fiancée, but they calmed him down, they reassured him. The rapidity with which the ceremony was going to be celebrated probably permitted him to escape the new law. Verlaine affirmed that he would submit quite voluntarily, once the marriage was celebrated, although under his breath he said "consummated." It was not serving the Fatherland that he feared, but seeing adjourned again and perhaps indefinitely, – for in the end, war is not a game, if one departed one might not return, – the hour so long anticipated of his promised happiness.

Verlaine had apprised me of his impatiences, of his agitation, and of his long passionate wait, but I had departed with the regiment, having enlisted at the moment of the declaration of war, a bit uncertain as to the conclusion of that marriage. The grave events like those that were in the works could have terrible repercussions on private interests.

I didn't attend the ceremony then, but I was there in spirit with the young newlyweds for, having been made aware of the celebration, despite its having been a thing of the past, I sent from the 13th corps of the army of the Rhine, to rue Lécluse, to the attention of M. Paul Verlaine, lyrical poet, and that of Mme. Paul Verlaine, a piece of verse, an epithalamion, which, if it arrived on time, remembered me to the two spouses, and marked my place among the attendees to the marriage, celebrated very simply moreover. The hour was tragic, and those were sinister auspices for their nuptials.

Verlaine's witnesses for the groom were Léon Valade and Paul Foucher. The ceremony took place at the Montmartre town hall, at the church of Notre-Dame de Clignancourt. In attendance, one noted the presence of a woman destined for a rather bitter celebrity, Louise Michel, then a teacher in Montmartre, and who was having a relationship with Verlaine's father-in-law, M. Mauté, cantonal delegate of the 18th arrondissement.

It was somber and blood red, Paul Verlaine's honeymoon. His nuptial song was drowned out by the noise of the cannons. The entrance into matrimony amidst a general disorder could only be followed by disarray. I have already mentioned the circumstances accompanying the double responsibilities that Verlaine had, both as a bureaucrat and a national guardsman, during the Siege and under the Commune. I have also noted the first disagreements that were developing in the young household, formed and developed by the ambient shocks and heartbreaks.

That lugubrious epoch is, however, captured in the literary history of the 19th century, in that of *The Good Song*.

The Good Song was composed during the winter of 1869 and the spring of 1870. The majority of the pieces that we know about, and doubtless also many that have disappeared, destroyed by the author or lost by the addressee, were addressed by Verlaine to his fiancée, during the two or three sojourns that she took in Normandy.

It comprises a very small number of short pieces, twenty-six poems.[7] It appeared during the war, – "a flower in a shell," as Victor Hugo said.

The original edition was printed on tinted Whatman paper, 32mo format. The cover contained this: "Paul Verlaine. The Good Song. The publisher's vignette. Paris. Alphonse Lemerre, publisher, passage Choiseul, 47, M.D.CCC.LXX." The volume contained 38 pages only. On the last page was this mention: "Printed on June 12, 1870, by L. Toinon et Company, for A. Lemerre, publisher in Paris."

We possess merely a selection of the tender and amorous pieces that Verlaine wrote during his feverish nuptial expectation.

Many from among these quasi improvisations, he said, were suppressed on submission of the definitive manuscript to Alphonse Lemerre, and I miss them, in all honesty, today... Those sacrificed pieces were certainly of equal merit to the others, and I have to ask

---

[7] twenty-six poems: twenty-one in the volume consulted for this book.

myself why that... perhaps puritanical... ostracism...
(*Confessions*. Second Part.)

Verlaine seems to indicate that he sacrificed those pieces on
account of their vivacity. They were however addressed to a young
girl, towards whom he observed the most extreme delicacy. One
conserved piece, with a rather hot tone to it, and which he declares
not to have sent to his innocent addressee until after he had attenuat-
ed it, with its too-characteristic traits effaced, prepared the fiancée
for the nuptial initiations. It evoked the instant

... where under my free hands finally
The powerless armor of the dress
And the fine linen will fall...

Alas! I should not have, added the poet, surprised ret-
rospectively by that scruple, *sung other Songs (for
ex.: Songs for Her, Odes in Her Honor), in which at
least the least hypocrisy, or to say it better, the least
restraint is, one might believe, carefully banished,
and regarding which I have nothing to repent, but
which, quite the contrary, succeed in awakening all,
or almost all, my desires in the flesh more ardently,
more fiercely now.*

Verlaine has testified on several occasions to his predilection
for that [original] collection [of poetry]. For starters, it was a testi-
mony of days of happiness. They are short. The others are also,
moreover. Those verses, amorously sincere, each time he recalled
them to memory, prolonged the ecstasy that he had, recalled to him
the escaped joys, made the clock of time resound the happy hours.
And that *Good Song,* it was Mathilde, it was his long loved, always
desired, and furiously missed wife, which reappeared in that poetic
vision, such as she appeared then in the enamored imagination of the
poet, adorned with all the qualities, all the goodness, loving, sweet,
docile, and all the more joyous by the happiness that she gave.

From the literary point of view, for us who do not have the
same visions to evoke and who would not know how to interest our-

selves in the subject per se, being preoccupied only in examining how the artist worked the delicate matter that he had undertaken to labor, we wouldn't know how to share in Verlaine's predilection.

What is of interest above all in that bouquet of marriage, the majority of whose flowers having been jealously withdrawn and kept to dry in the herbarium of memory, is that it demonstrates an entirely new poetic by him who fashioned it.

The Good Song, it is a transition piece, it is the passage from objective, descriptive, plastic, externalized poetry to personal expression, to a confession of the soul, to the notation of battles of the heart or excitations of the brain. It is the substitution of one art for another. To the cerebral visions; to the received, suggested, developed rather than felt, feelings; to the imagined passions; to the invented suffering; to the sensations that resulted from readings, conversations, hypotheses, rapprochements; succeed the personal, subjective, intimate, felt, lived, suffered poetry.

It is no longer the Victor Hugo of *The Legend of the Centuries*, but the poet of *Leaves of Autumn*,[8] and that of the *Contemplations,* whose influence will dominate from now on. The transformation begun, which the events were bound to bring to a head, and which, pursued partially in *Songs Without Words*, reached its goal in *Sagesse*, was due also to the penetration of certain personal poems by Mme. Desbordes-Valmore and Sainte-Beuve, writing under the pseudonym of Joseph Delorme. With what admiration, Paul cited fragments to me of that piece of such intense delicateness: "Always have I known her pensive and serious..."

Love, nuptial desire, the joy of confessing oneself, in that language of verse that he possessed better than others, the vulgar, and in which he felt more at ease, pushed him to that change in poetic manner. It was like a first conversion. We will see the new formula develop and become more precise, subsequently, which at that time was then more instinctive, as spontaneously generated and rising from events in his life, inspired by the contingencies of his amorous adventure. That cerebral mutation was at first an attempt, a preparation; it explains the coming metamorphosis of his intellectu-

[8]*Leaves of Autumn*: perhaps *Thoughts of Autumn*, by Sainte-Beuve.

ality, until then purely objective, from the point of view of sensations and affective desires.

At the hour when the poet was singing *The Good Song*, unforgettable hour that almost every one of us lived through, and which for us the poet specified the delights of, he abandoned the impersonal formula, he warbled for himself and for her, like a bird in the woods, egoistic musician, and seemed only concerned with being heard by those for whom his melodies mounted, like a jet of water, at night, among marbles.

What admirable fervor that was, that return to himself, that enthusiastic appeal to Beatrice, who was to guide him going forward and lead him out of the circles of Hell, where he felt himself precipitated, already half swallowed up:

As the dawn grows brighter, as behold the aurora!
As hope, after having fled me for a long time, really wants
To come back to me, who call it and who implore it,
As all this happiness really wants to be mine,

My mournful thoughts, they are behind me now,
They are behind me my bad dreams, ah! they are behind me
Above all the irony and pursed lips
And the words wherein my soulless mind triumphed.

Behind me also are my clenched fists and anger
With respect to the jerks and rascals I've encountered;
Behind me abominable rancor! behind me
The oblivion one seeks in execrable drinks!

Behold one of those cries à la Musset, – the poet so vehemently disdained by him, – the dead god that he wanted to knock down from his clay altar, one of those superhuman sobs that Verlaine will let out, subsequently, filled with despair and disgust, and which elicited from him then the desire for strolling happy and calm down the peaceable and regular path where "the finally-found companion" led him. Those there are the public displays of fervor, which demonstrate the profound and beneficial perturbation that had shaken his soul, in that spring full of storms and heavy with tempests in the fatal year 1870, the year that must be denominated Terrible, and which, for him, in the midst of the blasts of artilleries and the ruckus of empires bumping into each other in the blood-soaked mud, will remain the happy year, the blessed year, the excellent year of *The Good Song*.

He is sincere when he adds, the almost Christian vow, a resolution like something the young Levites might seize on as they prepare for ordination:

> *Yes, I want to walk straight and calm in Life,*
> *To the place where fate will lead my steps,*
> *Without violence, without remorse, without envy.*
> *It will be the happy duty in gay combats.*

He had hope, he had faith. Marriage was truly a sacrament for him. It was an initiation of the soul. He had never loved before, never been loved. He realized a dream that he had perhaps never had before. It was the most delicious moment of his existence. Subsequently, amidst the cries, blasphemies, canticles, elegies, invectives, hiccoughs, benedictions, and spasms, often in the ear of the damned and damning poet, the consoling rhythm, the divine ritornello will resonate:

> *How audacious! – a worthwhile price*
>
> *For his song, good or bad!*
> *But testifying, sincerely,*
> *Without* fadaise *and without false note,*
> *To the sweet malaise suffered in love.*

We will see now how fast the sky changed, and what night was formed in that sun-drenched soul of love, flowering with hope. Verlaine, in 1870, found everything beautiful, fine, good, when he had joy in his heart and love in his eyes. While rolling on the iron rails, in the somber plains of the North, he admired everything down to the very thin telegraph poles "whose wires look like paraphs, strangely" seen between the frame of the wagon's window curtains.

The smell of coal and water, the sound of the chains, the grating of the axles, all that was unable to trouble him in his contemplation of the white vision that made his heart joyous. The sound of the voice of the beloved blended in, in his mind, with the roaring sound of the brutal wagon, harmonizing it. In Paris, he found the route through the faubourg that he followed both noble and cheerful, among the sound of the cabarets, the filth of the sidewalks, the clanking storm of the omnibuses, the walls sweating with rain and moisture, the slippery pavement, the abominable course of the exterior boulevards, from Montmartre to Clignancourt, because he was going to a certain rendezvous, and paradise was at the other end of it. He believed in it, that paradise, and every one of us, more or less, one day and by whatever route he takes, will have seen that illusion. Verlaine's *The Good Song,* and that is the fine artistic title that he gave to it, is not an autobiography except in the details. It is a strophe detached from the eternal poem of youthful love, and for that reason it will endure.

Other Books by the Publisher

Fanchette's Pretty Little Foot by Restif de La Bretonne

Je M'Accuse... by Léon Bloy

My Hospitals & My Prisons by Paul Verlaine

Salvation Through the Jews by Léon Bloy

Words of a Demolitions Contractor by Léon Bloy

Cellulely by Paul Verlaine

Ecclesiastical Laurels by Jacques Rochette de la Morlière

Flowers of Bitumen by Émile Goudeau

Songs for Her & Odes in Her Honor by Paul Verlaine

On Huysmans' Tomb by Léon Bloy

Ten Years a Bohemian by Émile Goudeau

The Soul of Napoleon by Léon Bloy

Blood of the Poor by Léon Bloy

Joan of Arc and Germany by Léon Bloy

Theresa the Philosopher & The Carmelite Extern Nun by Marquis d'Argens & Anne-Gabriel Meusnier de Querlon

A Platonic Love by Paul Alexis

Two Novellas: Francine Cloarec's Funeral and Benjamin Rozes by Léon Hennique

The Revealer of the Globe: Christopher Columbus & His Future Beatification (Part One) by Léon Bloy

Héloïse Pajadou's Calvary by Lucien Descaves

An Immodest Proposal by Dr. Helmut Schleppend

The Pornographer by Restif de La Bretonne

Style (Theory and History) by Ernest Hello

On the Threshold of the Apocalypse: 1913-1915 by Léon Bloy

She Who Weeps (Our Lady of La Salette) by Léon Bloy

The Sylph by Claude Prosper Jolyot de Crébillon (*fils*)

School of Woman by Nicolas Chorier

Voyage in France by a Frenchman by Paul Verlaine

Ourigan, Oregon by William Clark, Richard Robinson, and anonymous

Drowning by Yu Dafu

Cull of April by Francis Vielé-Griffin

The Misfortune of Monsieur Fraque by Paul Alexis

Fêtes Galantes & Songs Without Words by Paul Verlaine

Joys by Francis Vielé-Griffin

The Son of Louis XVI by Léon Bloy

Septentrion by Jean Raspail

The Resurrection of Villiers de l'Isle-Adam by Léon Bloy

Poems Saturnian by Paul Verlaine

The Biography of Léon Bloy: Memories of a Friend by René Martineau

Fredegund, France: A Book of Poetry by Richard Robinson

www.ingramcontent.com/pod-product-compliance
Lightning Source LLC
Chambersburg PA
CBHW031447120626
46545CB00006B/2585